Have fun with
Arts and Crafts

Tractors and Trucks

Rita Storey

W
FRANKLIN WATTS
LONDON · SYDNEY

First published in 2012 by
Franklin Watts
338 Euston Road
London NW1 3BH

Franklin Watts Australia
Level 17/207 Kent Street
Sydney NSW 2000

Series editor: Amy Stephenson

Packaged for Franklin Watts by Storeybooks
rita@storeybooks.co.uk
Designer: Rita Storey
Editor: Nicola Barber
Crafts: Rita Storey
Photography: Tudor Photography, Banbury
www.tudorphotography.co.uk

A CIP catalogue record for this book is available
from the British Library.

Printed in China

Dewey classification: 745.5

ISBN 978 1 4451 1069 1

Cover images Wishlistimages (top left), Tudor Photography, Banbury

Franklin Watts is a division of Hachette Children's Books,
an Hachette UK company
www.hachette.co.uk

Before you start

Some of the projects in this book require scissors, paint, glue,
a sewing needle and a cooker. When using these things we
would recommend that children are supervised by
a responsible adult.

Newport Community Learning & Libraries
Cymuned ddysgu a Llyfrgelloedd Casnewydd

THIS ITEM SHOULD BE RETURNED OR
RENEWED BY THE LAST DATE
STAMPED BELOW

Malpas Library & Information Cent.
Tel: 656656

J

To renew telephone 656656 or 656657 (minicom)
or www.newport.gov.uk/libraries

Contents

Big Blue Tractor

Every farmer needs a strong tractor to do the hard work on the farm. A tractor is great for digging, pulling, lifting and pushing heavy loads. Make this bright blue tractor to drive around your farm.

To make a big blue tractor you will need

- 2 small rectangular cardboard boxes, 1 smaller than the other
- masking tape
- large sheet of paper
- felt-tip pen
- ruler
- scissors
- glue
- crayons
- black and blue paint and paintbrush
- 2 pairs of black lids – 1 pair larger than the other (you could use lids from soup containers and jam jars)
- coloured paper

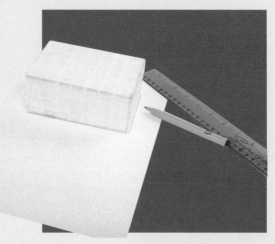

1 Tape all the flaps of the cardboard boxes closed. If the boxes are shiny, cover them with masking tape so that the paint will stick.

2 Place the larger of the two cardboard boxes on the paper with the biggest side facing up. Use the ruler and felt-tip pen to draw round the box. Do the same again and cut out the shapes. Leave these pieces of paper to one side.

3 Paint the boxes blue and leave them to dry.

4 Spread glue on to the long side of the small box. Glue the small box to the long, thin side of the larger box, near to the bottom.

5 While the paint is drying trim the pieces of paper (cut out in step 2) so that they narrow at the top. Using the crayons, draw a black line round the edge of each piece to look like tractor cab windows. Add controls like the ones above.

6 Glue the pieces of paper on to either side of the larger box.

7 Cut out four circles of coloured paper and glue one circle on to the centre of each lid.

9 Cut out a ladder and radiator grill shape from the paper left over in step 2. Paint the shapes black. Leave them to dry. Glue the radiator shape on to the front of the tractor. Glue the ladder on to one side of the tractor.

8 Spread glue on to the lids and stick them to the boxes to make wheels.

Chug, chug, chug, chug, chug, chug.

Terrific Tractors

Modern tractors are used to spray crops, sow seeds and pull mowers. They can also shift snow or piles of earth. Some tractors have huge wheels while others have crawlers, or caterpillar tracks around the wheels. Tractors are very good at driving across muddy or wet ground without getting stuck.

Dig It!

Tractors can have a whole variety of attachments for different jobs. The tractor in this picture has attachments that move just like the real thing. It has a bucket to scoop up earth or carry building materials, and a loader to push rocks and soil into a pile.

To make this tractor picture you will need

- felt-tip pen
- thin yellow card
- scissors
- glue
- thin black card
- thin red card
- glue
- 8 split pins

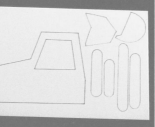

1 Using the felt-tip pen, draw the shapes of the tractor arms, bucket and loader on the yellow card. See pages 30 for the templates.

2 Cut out the shapes.

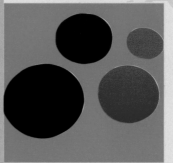

3 Using the templates on page 30, cut out two tractor wheels from the black card, one larger than the other, and two circles of red card smaller than the black circles.

4 Glue the red circles on to the middle of the black circles to make wheels.

5 Push a split pin through the centre of the larger of the wheels, then through the cab of the tractor just below the window. Open out the split pin.

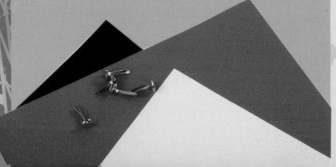

6 Push a split pin through the centre of the smaller wheel, then through the front of the tractor level with the back wheel. Open out the split pin.

7 Join the two pieces of the back arm together with a split pin.

8 Attach the bucket shape to the arm with a split pin.

9 Repeat stages 7 and 8 with the front arm and loader attachment.

10 Using a split pin, attach the front arm to the front of the tractor.

11 Using a split pin, attach the back arm to the back of the tractor.

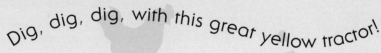

Dig, dig, dig, with this great yellow tractor!

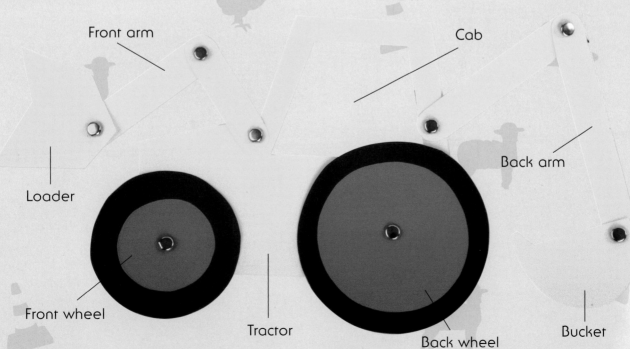

Front arm

Cab

Loader

Back arm

Front wheel

Tractor

Back wheel

Bucket

7

Working in the Fields

Y ou will often see tractors pulling ploughs in the countryside. Imagine a country scene with lots of little fields – all different colours and textures. Decorate your fields with different patterns and set your toy tractors to work in them.

To make a textured field picture you will need

- A3 sheet of thick paper cut into 12 squares, 99mm x 105mm
  - paints and paintbrushes
    - glue
    - seeds, sand, leaves
  - green and yellow tissue paper
    - cotton wool
    - felt-tip pen
    - netting
- sheet of thick paper larger than A3

1 Paint the squares of thick paper in shades of green and brown. Leave them to dry. Decorate each piece with a different field pattern.

2 Spread glue on to a green background either in lines or all over. Scatter seeds on the glue and tap any remaining seeds off.

3 Screw up small pieces of green tissue paper. Glue them in lines on a brown background to look like crops or along the edges of the fields to make hedges.

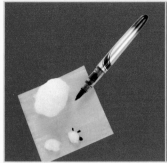

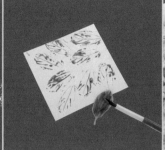

4 Roll small pieces of cotton wool into balls and glue them on to a green square. Draw legs and a face with a felt-tip pen to look like sheep.

5 Paint three wavy lines or three diagonal lines of glue on to a brown background. Scatter sand on to the glue. Tip off any sand that does not stick.

6 Paint the back of a leaf and print it on to a yellow background.

7 Small pieces of yellow tissue paper screwed into balls make good sunflowers.

8 Glue strips of netting round a green square to look like fences around a meadow.

9 Glue all the squares onto a large sheet of thick paper.

10 Can you think of anything else to use to make crop textures?

Watch your toy tractors hard at work in the fields.

Tractor Tyre Tracks

Tractors have thick tyres that can grip in mud, or on snow and ice. The tyres have different patterns on their treads. You can make your own tyre treads to print a great tractor tyre pattern picture.

To make a tractor tyre picture you will need

- felt-tip pen
- scissors
- sheet of foam
- A4 sheets of thick paper (white or coloured)
- cardboard tube from the inside of a kitchen roll
- glue
- paintbrush
- sticky tape
- baking tray
- scrap of cardboard
- paint
- scrap paper
- large sheet of white paper

1 Using the templates on page 31, copy the shapes and draw them on to the sheet of foam with a felt-tip pen. Cut out the shapes.

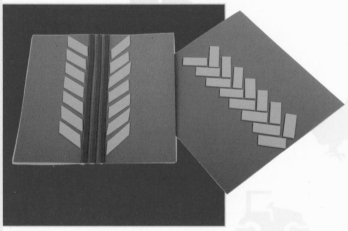

2 Cut a piece of thick paper narrower than the length of the cardboard tube and wide enough to wrap round it. Brush some glue on to the back of each shape and glue them on to the paper in a pattern like the ones in the picture above. Leave to dry.

3 With the shapes on the outside, roll the paper round the tube and secure with sticky tape.

4 Using the scrap of cardboard, spread a thin layer of paint in the baking tray.

5 Roll the tube in the paint.

6 Roll the tube on to the scrap paper to get rid of excess paint. Print a tyre track on to the large sheet of paper. Leave to dry.

7 Repeat stages 1 – 6 with a different pattern and colour. Build up a colourful tyre track picture. You can print as many tracks in as many colours as you like. For each set of tracks use a different pattern (see stages 2 – 3).

Vroom, vroom, vrooooommmmm.

Lorry Cab

To make the dashboard of a 'big rig' grab a large cardboard box and some paint, then use your imagination to find odds and ends that can be used to make levers, buttons, joysticks and switches. Drive your 'big rig' anywhere you like!

To make a dashboard you will need

- large cardboard box
- scissors
- paint and paintbrush
- sticky tape
- black poster board
- compass and pencil
- ruler
- cardboard tube
- glue
- soup container lid
- a selection of lids and tops from bottles or herb jars
- coloured paper
- telephone cable
- matchbox

1 Open out the cardboard box and cut off the top. Cut off one side. Paint the inside of the box.

2 Pull the sides towards each other so that they are at an angle to the middle section. Tape in place. Bend back the top third.

3 Set the compass to 12cm and draw a circle on the black poster board. Keep the point in the same place but change the compass to 8cm. Draw another circle inside the first. Keep the point in the same place but change the compass to 3.5cm. Draw another circle inside the first two. Cut round the largest circle line.

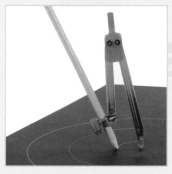

4 Lay the ruler with the end on the small circle. Draw a line on either side of it. Repeat twice more evenly spaced round the wheel. The lines you draw should make the shape of a big 'Y'. Cut out between the lines as shown here.

5 Cut one end off the cardboard tube at an angle. Cut slits 1cm long and 5mm apart all the way round both ends. Bend back the tabs.

   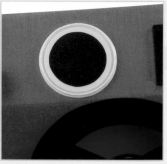

6 Paint the tube black. Glue the tabs on the straight end of the tube to the back of the steering wheel.

7 Sread glue on to the tabs on the angled end of the tube.

8 Position the steering wheel on the base of the box so that the wheel is angled towards you. Glue a circle of coloured paper to a jam jar lid to make a horn. Glue it to the centre of the wheel.

9 Use the compass to draw a circle on the black paper the size of the inner circle of the soup container. Cut out the circle and glue it on to the lid. Brush glue on to the back of the lid and glue it on to the dashboard to make a speedometer.

10 If you can find an old piece of telephone cable, attach a matchbox to the end with tape. Paint the matchbox black and you have a CB radio handset.

11 Glue circles of coloured paper to the tops from used herb jars. Glue them on to the dashboard to make buttons. Add card shapes to to make panels, speakers or displays for your dashbard.

Hi, Good Buddy!

Citizen Band radio (CB for short) is a way that truckers talk to each other from their cabs. Rather than using their real names, CB radio users have 'handles' (nicknames). They also have lots of unusual words and expressions for CB radio – read some of them in the CB Radio Glossary on page 32.

Magnetic Tractor Game

Tractors work hard pulling ploughs and carrying heavy loads round farms. How quickly can your tractor get a bale of hay to the sheep in the furthest field?

To make a magnetic tractor game you will need

- pair of magnets
- ruler
- toy tractor
- A3 piece of cardboard
- paint or felt-tip pens
- 4 bottle tops (all the same size)
- glue
- watch or stopwatch
- small sweets or toy hay bale

To make each sheep

- square of thin card 8cm x 8cm
- glue
- cotton wool ball
- googly eye

Board

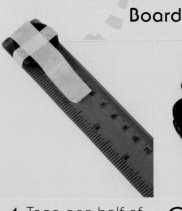

1 Tape one half of the magnet to the end of the ruler.

2 Tape the other half of the magnet underneath the tractor.

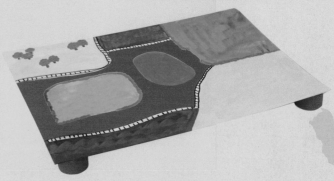

3 Draw or paint a farm track just wider than the tractor on to the cardboard. Include some tight turns. Paint the farm around the track. Glue the four bottle tops to the underside of the track, one in each corner.

Sheep

4 Fold the square of card in half. Draw your sheep on the card, making sure 2cm of the back of the sheep is along the fold at the top. Cut out your sheep, but don't cut along the fold.

5 Pull the cotton wool ball in half. Glue half of the cotton wool ball on to each side of the body of the sheep. Glue on a googly eye. Make as many sheep as you need.

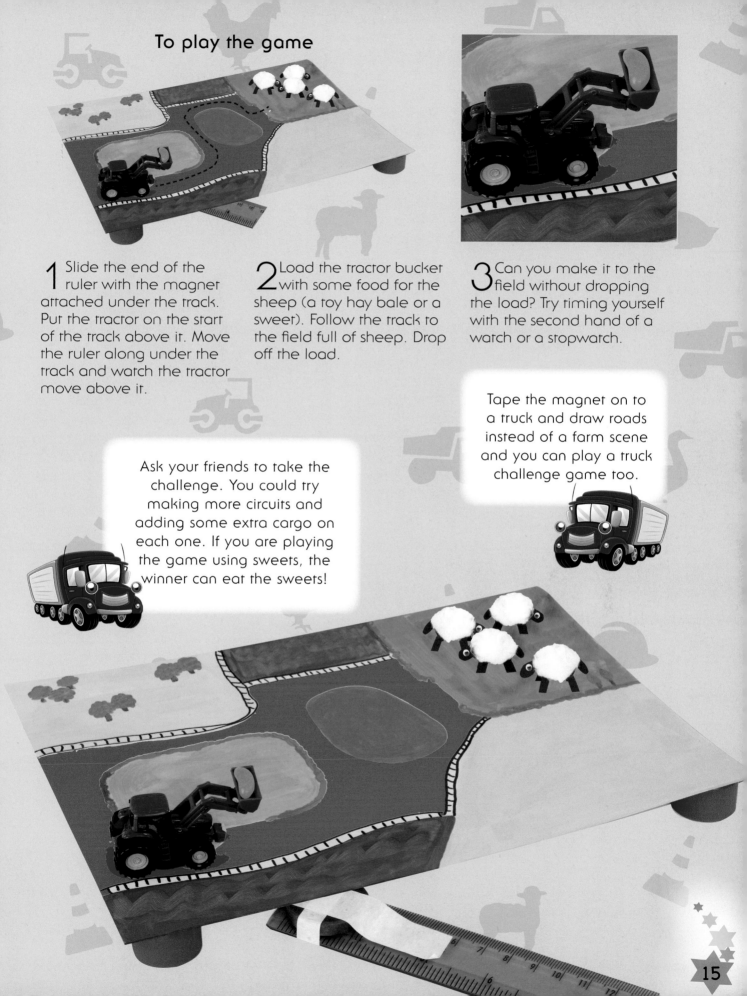

To play the game

1 Slide the end of the ruler with the magnet attached under the track. Put the tractor on the start of the track above it. Move the ruler along under the track and watch the tractor move above it.

2 Load the tractor bucket with some food for the sheep (a toy hay bale or a sweet). Follow the track to the field full of sheep. Drop off the load.

3 Can you make it to the field without dropping the load? Try timing yourself with the second hand of a watch or a stopwatch.

Tape the magnet on to a truck and draw roads instead of a farm scene and you can play a truck challenge game too.

Ask your friends to take the challenge. You could try making more circuits and adding some extra cargo on each one. If you are playing the game using sweets, the winner can eat the sweets!

Notebook Truck Graphics

Trucks are often covered in colourful and sometimes crazy graphics. Create your own zany graphic sign and turn a plain notebook into a really funky one.

To make notebook truck graphics you will need

- sheet of white paper
- sheet of coloured paper the same size as your notebook
- felt-tip pens
- scissors
- crayons
- newspapers and magazines
- glue
- stick-on stars
- notebook
- clear adhesive film

1 On a sheet of paper draw some flames the width of the paper. See page 30 for a template to copy. Using crayons, colour in the flames.

2 Lots of truck graphics include an animal. Cut out a picture from a magazine or draw one on coloured paper. Cut out a circle around the animal. Cut out a truck from a magazine or draw one of your own.

3 Glue the flames onto the sheet of coloured paper. Glue the circle containing the animal near the top of the flames. Glue the truck at the bottom. Leave to dry.

4 Cut round the edge of the shape. Follow the shape but leave a border all the way round.

Truck Wraps

The amazing graphics on trucks and trailers are often designed on a computer and printed out onto sheets of thin sticky-backed vinyl. The printed sheets are carefully stuck onto each panel of the truck or trailer.

5 Glue the shape to the front of a notebook. Finish your picture by sticking on some stars. Cover the picture with clear adhesive film.

Milk Tanker

Milk tankers collect fresh milk from farms every day. They take it to a big depot where it is treated. Some of it is put into cartons, ready to go to the supermarket. You can make this milk tanker ready for the next milk collection.

To make a milk tanker you will need

- large cardboard crisp tube
- sheet of white paper as wide as the tube and long enough to wrap round it
- sticky tape
- sheet of coloured paper as wide as the tube and long enough to wrap half way round it
- scissors
- pencil
- black paint and paintbrush
- glue
- 2 elastic bands
- 5 small cardboard tubes
- black paper
- small cardboard box
- red paint and paintbrush
- silver paper
- white paper
- felt-tip pen

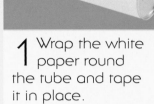

1 Wrap the white paper round the tube and tape it in place.

2 Using the template on pages 31 cut both the long edges of the coloured paper into a curved shape.

3 Glue the coloured paper on to the tube. Hold in place with two elastic bands. When the glue is dry. remove the elastic bands.

4 Draw round the end of the small cardboard tube on to the black paper. Repeat ten times. Cut out each circle 2mm wider than the circles you have drawn.

5 Paint the tubes black. Leave to dry.

6 Paint glue on to the top edge of one of the tubes.

7 Press the glued edge on to a circle of paper. Do the same on the other end. Repeat with the rest of the tubes.

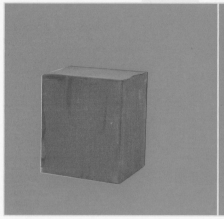
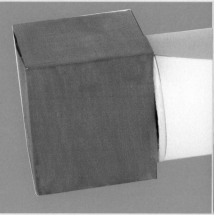
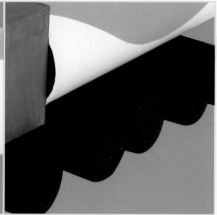

8 Paint the small box red. Leave to dry.

9 Glue one end of the large tube to the box.

10 Glue the small tubes to the bottom of your tanker. Glue one tube under the cab and two pairs under the large tube.

11 Cut ten circles of silver paper and glue one in the middle of each wheel. Leave everything to dry.

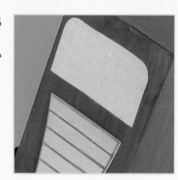

12 Cut out the shape of a windscreen and a front grill from white paper (like the ones on the milk tanker below). Draw horizontal lines on the front grill with a felt-tip pen.

With this smart milk tanker you are ready to hit the road.

Car Transporter

Car transporters deliver new cars all over the country. The back of this model car transporter folds down so that you can drive your toy cars up the ramp. Fill it up and make an express delivery.

To make this car transporter you will need

- shoe box with lid
- scissors
- duct tape
- paint
- paintbrush
- coloured paper
- black and red card
- glue

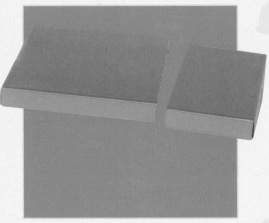

1 Cut across the lid of the shoe box, one-third of the way along.

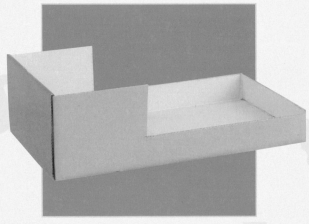

2 Cut a section out of the shoe box. It needs to be the same length as the long piece of the lid. Cut two-thirds of the way down the box and then along to the end.

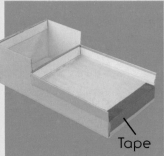

Tape

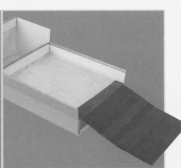

3 Turn the larger section of lid round and attach the cut end to the back of the transporter with sticky tape.

4 Trim one of the pieces of card that was cut from the side of the box to be the same width as the lid. Tape it on to the back of the lorry to make a ramp.

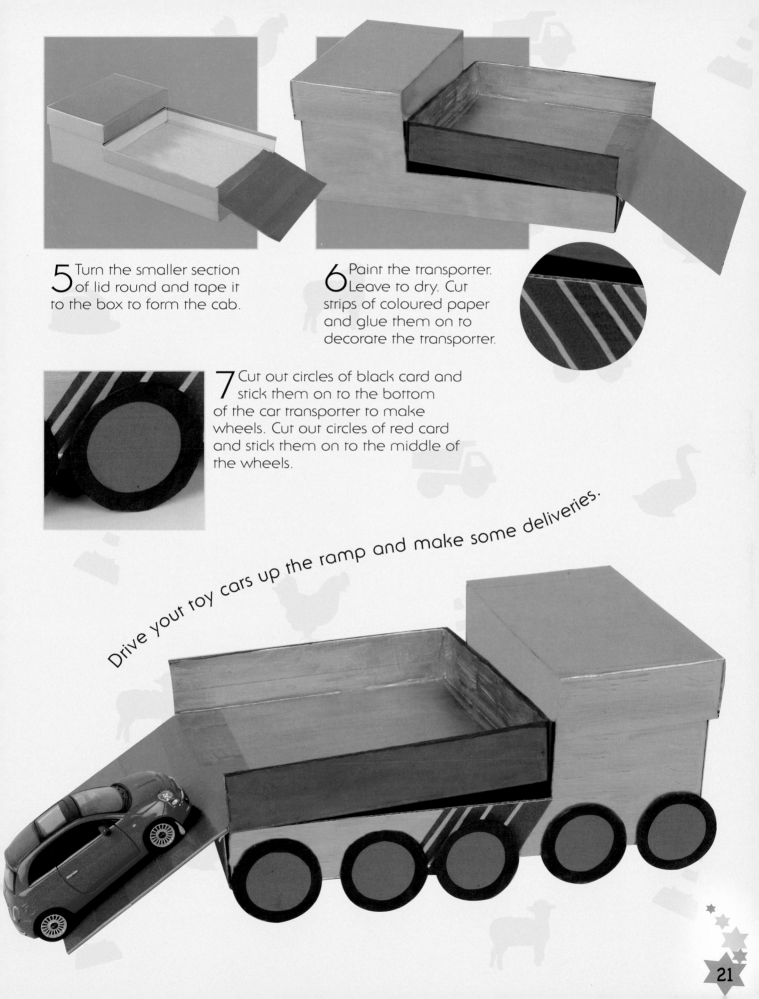

5 Turn the smaller section of lid round and tape it to the box to form the cab.

6 Paint the transporter. Leave to dry. Cut strips of coloured paper and glue them on to decorate the transporter.

7 Cut out circles of black card and stick them on to the bottom of the car transporter to make wheels. Cut out circles of red card and stick them on to the middle of the wheels.

Drive your toy cars up the ramp and make some deliveries.

Trucker's Lunch

Truckers need a good packed lunch to keep them going on those long journeys. Make yourself a tasty trucker's lunch.

To make a trucker's lunch you will need

Truck rolls

- 2 white bread rolls • butter • knife
- 2 slices of cheese or ham
- 6 cherry tomatoes
- 6 slices of cucumber
- 6 cocktail sticks (with the sharp ends removed)

Traffic light fruit kebabs

- 3 red fruits – grapes, strawberries or cherries (stones removed)
- 3 orange fruits – orange segments or cubes of melon
- 3 green fruits – grapes or slices of kiwi
- 3 cocktail sticks (with the sharp ends removed)
- kitchen knife

Rocky road

- 125g butter
- 300g milk chocolate, broken into pieces
- 3 tbsp golden syrup
- 200g digestive biscuits
- 100g mini marshmallows
- icing sugar
- bowl • saucepan • wooden spoon
- plastic bag • rolling pin
- baking tin, 24cm x 15cm
- spatula • kitchen knife

A Truck Roll

1 Slice both of the rolls in half lengthways and spread both halves with butter. Place the ham or cheese slices on to one half of the roll. Put the top half of the roll on top of the filling.

2 Cut the rolls two thirds of the way along. Cut the cucumber slices in half. Cut the tomatoes in half through the middle.

Take out the cocktail sticks when you serve the rolls.

3 Thread a half cucumber slice and half a tomato on to a cocktail stick and push the cocktail stick through the rolls. Push a slice of cucumber and a tomato on the other side. Repeat with all the tomatoes and cucumber to make three sets of wheels for your truck roll.

Traffic Light Fruit Kebabs

1 To make a red–orange–green traffic light, thread a red fruit, an orange fruit and a green fruit on to a cocktail stick.

Rocky Road

1 Put the butter chocolate pieces, and golden syrup in to a bowl. Put some water into the saucepan. Rest the bowl on the saucepan. The bowl must not touch the water. Put the pan on to a low heat. Stir with a wooden spoon until everything is melted. Take the pan off the heat.

Ask an adult to help you with step 1 of the Rocky Road recipe.

2 Put the biscuits into a plastic bag and tap the bag gently with the rolling pin until there are some crumbs and a few larger chunks of biscuit.

3 Tip the melted chocolate mixture into a bowl. Tip the biscuit pieces and crumbs into the melted mixture. Add the marshmallows. Stir everything together.

4 Tip the mixture into a baking tin and smooth the top with the wooden spoon. Put the tray in to the fridge for 2 – 3 hours. When the mixture has set, cut into squares and sprinkle with icing sugar.

Monster Truck Driver

If you want to drive a truck of your own, now is your chance. Find a picture of yourself and put it in the driving seat of this cool monster truck card.

To make this truck card you will need

- A4 sheet of stiff paper
- scissors
- masking tape
- card
- thick paints and stiff paintbrushes
- felt-tip pens
- glitter glue
- small photograph of yourself to put in the driver's seat

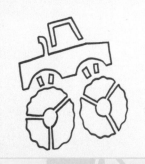

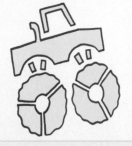

1 Trace the shape on page 31 on to a sheet of stiff paper.

2 Cut out the sections shown in blue to create a truck stencil (this is a bit fiddly so ask an adult to help).

3 Using masking tape, tape the stencil to a sheet of card so that the stencil covers the bottom half of the card.

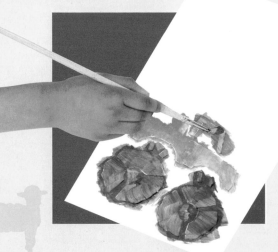

4 Use thick paint and a stiff brush to paint through the stencil on to the card.

5 Carefully peel off the stencil. When it is dry you can use the same stencil again to print another card.

6 Fold the card in half so that the fold is at the top.

7 Use felt-tip pens and glitter glue to decorate your truck.

8 Cut out your photo to fit in the cab window. Glue it in to the window.

Make a card for a friend so that they can be a monster truck driver too!

Monster Truck Stunt Game

In this monster truck stunt game you can drive your own monster truck round a crazy track. Challenge a friend to play and 'put the pedal to the metal' in a race for the finish line – doing some amazing freestyle stunts on the way.

To make and play the monster truck stunt game you will need

- coloured paper
- coin
- felt-tip pen
- scissors
- A3 sheet of card
- glue
- thick white paper
- crayons
- dice

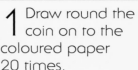

1 Draw round the coin on to the coloured paper 20 times.

2 Cut out the circles.

3 Glue the coloured circles on to the coloured card. The circles need to touch but can make a wiggly line going across the board.

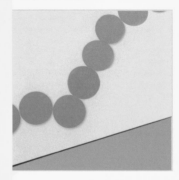

4 Draw flashes like the ones shown. Colour them with the crayons. Cut them out and glue them on to as many circles as you want. Make sure you glue one on circle number 20.

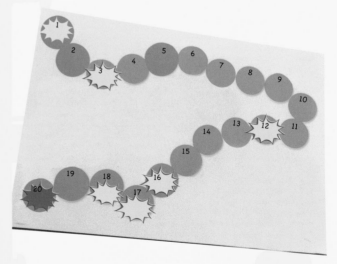

5 Number the circles 1– 20 as shown, from top left. Decorate the board with cut out monster truck pictures. Write 'Winner' on circle 20.

6 Write instructions on the circles and flashes. Use these or think up some of your own

- jump 3 cars (move forward 3 spaces)
- squash 2 cars (miss a turn)
- crazy crash but keep going (miss a turn)
- flip the truck (move to the next circle)
- wipe out. Game over!

7 To make the counters: draw round the coin onto the thick white paper until you have one circle for each player. Cut the circles out. Draw a monster truck on each counter, each one a different colour, or cut out trucks from a magazine and glue them on.

Go to www.franklinwatts. co.uk for some pictures to download or copy.

Monster Trucks

Monster trucks are customised trucks with huge wheels and crazy graphics. They race, jump, crush cars, perform freestyle displays and other crazy stunts.

How to play the game

Each player has a counter and puts it on the first circle. The first player rolls the dice. Move the counter the number of circles shown on the dice. If there is an instruction on the circle, do as it says. Take it in turns to throw the dice. The winner is the first one to reach the finish line by throwing the exact number to land on circle 20.

Mosaic Pictures

Build mosaic pictures of a fire engine and a colourful tractor. They will look great on your bedroom wall.

To make mosaic pictures you will need

Fire engine

- sheets of red, black, yellow and orange paper
- scissors
- yellow background paper
- glue
- brush

Tractor

- sheets of yellow, black, red, brown and cream paper
- scissors
- purple background paper
- glue
- brush

1 Cut the red paper into strips 1cm wide.

2 Cut the strips into lots of squares 1cm x 1cm.

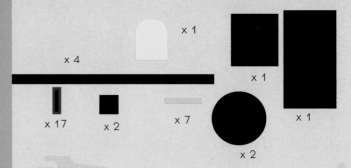

x 1

x 4

x 17   x 2   x 7   x 1   x 1

x 2

3 Copy the shapes above and cut them out to make the ladders, wheels, doors, windows and bumpers.

3 Lay the squares on to a piece of paper so that they build up a picture of a tractor. Add a dab of glue on to the back of each piece and glue in position on the picture.

Keep the paper on a flat surface and away from any draughts until you have glued all the squares in place.

Tractor

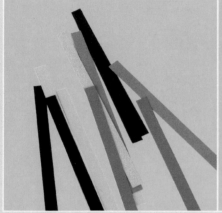

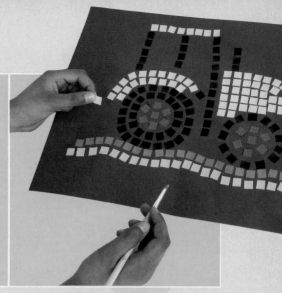

1 Cut the coloured paper into strips 1cm wide.

2 Cut the strips into lots of squares 1cm x 1cm.

3 Lay the squares on to a piece of paper so that they build up a picture of a tractor. Add a dab of glue on to the back of each piece and glue in position on the picture.

Give your tractor a name and make the name part of your mosaic.

Templates

Dig It!
Pages 6 – 7

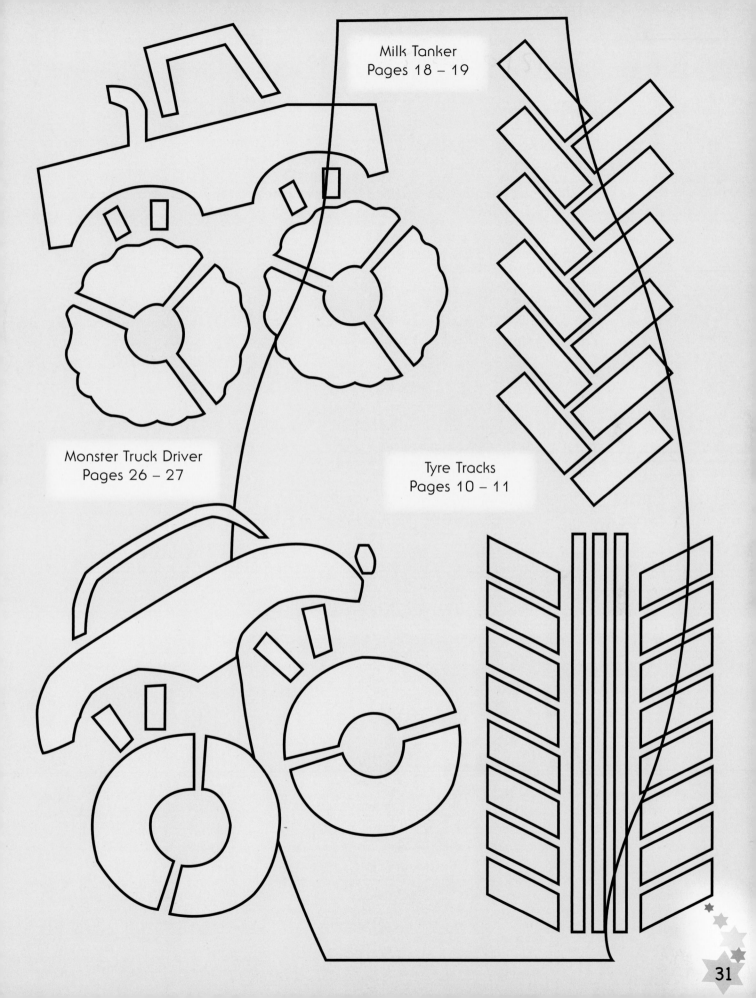

Milk Tanker
Pages 18 – 19

Monster Truck Driver
Pages 26 – 27

Tyre Tracks
Pages 10 – 11

31

CB Radio Glossary

Good buddy a friendly greeting when talking to other CB radio users
Bearmobile police car
Bear in the air police helicopter
Big rig 18-wheel truck
Do you copy? do you understand?
Breaker 19 what you would say to other users when you want to use the channel
Your handle the nickname you use when using a CB radio
Put the pedal to the metal accelerate
10 4 message received

Phonetic Alphabet

Not all truckers use this alphabet but it helps to spell things out on a crackly radio hook-up. Can you spell out your name using the alphabet below?

Lucy = Lima – Uniform – Charlie – Yankee
Sam = Sierra – Alpha – Mike

A = Alpha	J = Juliet	S = Sierra
B = Bravo	K = Kilo	T = Tango
C = Charlie	L = Lima	U = Uniform
D = Delta	M = Mike	V = Victor
E = Echo	N =November	W = Whiskey
F = Foxtrot	O = Oscar	X = X-ray
G = Golf	P = Papa	Y = Yankee
H = Hotel	Q = Quebec	Z = Zulu
I = India	R = Romeo	

Further Information

Books
Machines at Work: Tractors by Clive Gifford (Wayland, 2012)

Machines On The Move: Tractors by James Nixon (Franklin Watts, 2011)
Machines On The Move: Trucks by James Nixon (Franklin Watts, 2011)

Machines Rule: series by Steve Parker (Franklin Watts, 2011)

Motorsports: Monster Trucks by Clive Gifford (Franklin Watts, 2012)

Websites
http://www.playtruckgames.org/

Index